Happenings, Heartbeats,

and Mental Breakdowns

Poems

by

M. B. Manthe

Lighted Lake Press

Happenings, Heartbeats, and Mental Breakdowns

Copyright © 2015 by M. B. Manthe
All rights reserved.

Suggested cataloging data:

Manthe, M. B., 1971-
Happenings, heartbeats, and mental breakdowns: poems /
      by M. B. Manthe.

1. Depression, Mental — Poetry.
2. Man-woman relationships — Poetry.
3. Young women — Poetry.
4. Grief — Poetry.
5. American poetry — 21st century.

PS3613.A5784 H36 2015
811'.6 — dc23

ISBN 13: 978-0-9969627-0-4
LCCN: 2015917705

Lighted Lake Press
Topeka, KS

For Jeff, Kyle, and Ryan.

You mean the world to me,
even though you sometimes
drive me crazy.

Love you.

Road Work	1
A Light Heart	2
Nighttime on 95	3
Break of Dawn	4
Half the Basement Stairs	5
Weight	6
Here	8
Watching from a Darkened House	9
Cast Party	10
Dissociation	11
Catalina	12
"You're the ocean," he said.	14
Beavertail	15
Newport	16
A Box, a Life	17
(Untitled)	18
Demons	19
Underwater Thing	21
A Slice of Otto B.	22
Waterfall	23
Cages	24

Apples and Hot Chocolate...26

Broken Glass ... Madness..27

Wild..28

Happier Time...29

Electrical Storm..30

The Walk..31

Romance 33

Snow Shovels...34

Losing Everything but Our Appetites................................35

The End of the Story for the Lover of Books 44

Me, My Dad, and Patty Griffin...45

Schism..46

Asylum...47

A Little Piece 48

Snow Day 49

Baptism 50

One Thousand Thousand..51

Tank...54

Corner Story 55

The Breaking 56

Children's Television..57

Universal Event	59
One Evening	60
A Family's Fences	61
My Home	62
Redcoat Lane	63
An Attempt at Prayer	64
Rocks and a Newport Shore	66
A Breath Returning	68
No Sunrise	69
Road Blocks	70
Notes on the Poems	71
Acknowledgments	73
About the Author	77

Road Work

Sometimes I think summer has its own
pattern after all, some weirdly repeated

series of actions, happenings, heartbeats,
and mental breakdowns. I'm standing

on a rainbow at night, watching you rush
through life as if it were a brainless

board game, no more than a day job
or an ex-girlfriend's favorite song.

You don't understand color, that your eyes
aren't sexy because they are

shimmering lighted-lake blue
but because they are so much darling you.

Every day I close my eyes and thank God
you have no feelings. But maybe

I imagine you — the strange music you love
that no one plays on the radio, your body

I love, pizzas we share in front of the television,
even your house, maybe all of this

is false, filled with helium and blowing off.
Tonight is hot and calling after me, "Marie."

It's hell to move around. We're all sweating
and they're tearing everything up.

A Light Heart

Beneath the string, the ribbons tied
to a helium heart that rubs the roof,
there sits an empty bed — untouched,
perfectly made with twin sheets
of navy, feminine flowered spread,
separate from the milk-white walls
and bare floors.
     The heart is half red,
half silver, filled with liquid warmth,
passed from one to another.
It is the room's center, swayed
in the air by cool currents, hot streaks,
and volcanic beating within.
It is above everything.
      Soft sounds
echo from hours ago, when she rose
early, readied herself for work,
bustled about after the shower. The house
still sleeps as she eats: cold cereal, milk,
bright schoolhouse apple — her habits
stagnate in the darkness of childhood,
the unlit kitchen where she eats.

Nighttime on 95

Their bright pinpricks
follow me at night.
Sharp, white, reflected in my face
until I'm blind,
glowing eyes chase
me through one-way darkness.
Faster! Faster!
My foot takes me further away,
I fly.
Still, the shining circles
come closer …
Closer!

Everyone passes me.

Break of Dawn

The Earth's own color, its only genuine shade, is gray
against the constant nighttime of inner space,
a black and cool — but sometimes starry — wrap
around the global town. The loss of leaves
and sun brings too much sorrow to say —
my breath slows, my blood waits for light.

But then again, December.
A few at first, and more before long, building
the city of light. The trees and stars are pulled down
and put to use in the people's houses. Outside,
strings of lights proclaim the month of wonder:
December opens hearts, brings them to bloom.
The candles and Santas, the stars and menorahs,
even the desk light shining upon this page
as I wait and consider on the eve of December,
all together, they are the choir
of the city of light — sharing life, speaking hope, rejoicing.

Half the Basement Stairs

The moon hangs at half-mast.
Nights on the stairs are in my head,
the stairs I don't dare return to.
Often, the music was loud, and I sat invisibly,
as much wood as a table, and content.
My blood and shoulders moved, my eyes
watched the walls and the time,
watched all the music go by.

This evening's moon is half a face.
I remember the fingers and mouths,
the strings that I felt, and the sounds.
The air glittered — its own combustion —
and I took in the flame
like the frozen woman I was.
Wires were melting; I breathed.

Exactly half the moon has been eaten.
Half my night is missing;
I am doing nothing, alone.
This is fine
with me, the way I want to be,
yet I miss the freedom
of sitting between the shadows and blending in.
I've lost my place on
the stairs, and I can't hear a thing.

Weight

In college, there was a poster
stuck up on the living room wall
depicting women of all sizes and shapes
floating, drifting across the sky.
"Celebrate your natural sizes," it said.
When Lori and I considered this message,
my response was quick, and practical:
"But I can't fit into my natural clothes!"
This is only one moment from the ongoing story
of extra weight — so rarely lost,
and far too often found.

At full term with my first son, I weighed
one hundred ninety-seven pounds;
with my second, two hundred ten.
It's difficult to comprehend
having a second belly, one that kicks.
During the third trimester, I carried
a weight I could never put down.
Such exquisite relief I felt
when the doctor lifted my firstborn from me;
I was instantly, refreshingly lighter.

Last evening, my second son,
almost four, fell asleep on the drive
to the library. I unbuckled him,
put his lollipop in my mouth, picked up
his heavy sleeping weight, his head
almost slipping off my shoulder.
Inside the building — blessedly cool
on the hottest day of the year —
I dropped off our videos, and threw
the lollipop away. I quickly found the book
I wanted, brought it and my son

to the self-checkout. I imagined myself
laying him down at my feet,
but I didn't. I juggled my wallet,
my library card, the book, and my kid,
then took everything out into the heat.
My shirt had scooted up my tummy,
and Ryan's shirt was higher still.
My arms were weakening, my mind
recalling a pregnant belly, the weight
I could never put down.
My sleeping son is no longer
that same bundle of joy, but a boy
who's been calling me "Pretty Mommy."
I open the door, and gently put him down.
I start the car, then softly strap in
my handsome son, this wondrous, precious weight.

Here

I am alone here. The sky
opens wide on me,
lets fly its angry lightning,
flash after ominous flash against
the dark, while I walk
quickly beneath the split
black sheets, the air above
coming into my clothes
thick and heavy on my
skin, the same air
that hides the stars.

I'm almost used to it:
I've been cut like this before.
The sound of a whirring knife
is born inside my mind, a tangle
of voices brings me to shame,
and I relearn my own
capacity for rage. This sound
begins to breathe, spinning
until my head's waving side
to side, crying, crying out, and
I'm flipping slipping going
gone to where no one
no one can touch me.

Alone here, I am trying
to hold myself. My arms
are shaking and warm, hands
unsure, wet with tears, but
loving, reaching, sincere.

Watching from a Darkened House

They flesh out pages, fatten words
of dialogue spoken only
by the blackest ink.
Standing, always facing out,
actors create life from legend,
singing an era with a gesture.
Then the house goes dark, and the
horror of offstage life
overwhelms them like confetti.

You can see it in
between-scene expressions,
that they are still children
playing dress-up with personality,
parading the big put-on,
the charade of adulthood.
When the house goes dark, reality
bleeds into their souls like glass.
They make their peace with the sunrise.

Cast Party

There's that relief, you know,
when it goes,
floats off like a boat

on playful water.
The closing note
is sung, the work is done.

But were the months
worth a two-night high,
dinner on the floor,

a little laughter,
with hysteria blown in
to even the measure?

It's over. The cry
from my throat and my eyes
is the sound of goodbye.

Dissociation

I'm starting to thicken now,
to wax and harden.
I overfill and casually spill,
wanting to tear myself down.

This skin is the newest thing:
a smooth glitter, unbreaking.
It began in my mouth
like a sentence, and grew on.

Such distance, dislocation,
a cold and sterile place.
There are walls and chairs
with hands and faces

in the black and white
of a black afternoon.
The papery crowd
knocks about, unhurt.

A chill is all I feel.
Water waves around me.
My eyes are out,
spent as old nickels.

Meanwhile, I'm starting to thicken.

Catalina

The sun beats into the skin of the desert
flowers. The Catalinas glow golden

and warm, north of my home.
They seem to call me to them, holding up

pieces of the life I left, the girl
I was. The desert's making room for me.

Back in Massachusetts, my mother
has been in the house the three months

since I left. If I could see her,
perhaps she would remind me who

I am. I'm often alone now, some days
so baked by the light I can't think.

I remember a boy I loved once, his eyes
and lips like the sky, and I see

him every day in the face of the mountains
north of my home, glowing golden, turning

pink, then dark. I wonder at my heart,
gone dry and bare; I wonder that

the moon is everywhere. I've forgotten what
I used to mean, and what

I used to dream. I imagine now
that mountains call, that old friends

think of me, and I make plans —
I imagine it all. Really, where I am

is a room, nothing else. I pretend
it's a seashell in the desert: on quiet

nights, I listen, missing the life
I left — myself, most of all.

"You're the ocean," he said.

So it's you, again,
forgetting the vast
wet ocean flares
heavy in her rage,
unrolls stormy tides
on the heads of
thoughtless men, yet spares
all women in love.

And so you come,
not thinking you
are the last thing I want
or need, now.
You walk me through
the jungle, start again
on a shore so new
it makes me love
you — again.

I wish I'd seen
the full moon
before I saw you …
ah, my blood
flows cool and sweet,
my legs have shaken
off the heat.

My eyes and arms
reflect the stars;
heaven can hold you,
wherever you are.

Beavertail

A dark and narrow road
lined with wildflowers unfolded
before us. The lighthouse
played tricks in my face,
its flashes steady, electric,
hot waves splitting air
and my sleepy head — what a shock!
That path curved into my heart.

We stopped to share a sky of stars.
The stars! — more brilliant than any
I've known since I was eight.
Then, I loved my father,
his talk of history and astronomy,
his youth in New York City.
I'm still learning all that,
still building me.

And he — my friend at Beavertail —
moved in closer even while
he spoke. The night tides broke
a thousand times out there,
rhythm of the water's surface
smooth as his hands on my back.
I never dreamed I'd be in this.

Yet I gave up
nothing. I am, as then.

Newport

If you love me as you say,
take me to Newport again
to gaze at the sea and then
to soak in the sun all day,
feeling the power in each ray
as it beats on me. In ten
years it will look like heaven,
when we turn to our past, this way,
to Newport. I wonder how
time will affect our faces —
will he put lines on my brow,
and steal your precious graces?
And most — what will become of
the Newport I so much love?

A Box, a Life

The box she lives in
Is shaken with blaring sounds:
Radio, television —
Chaos never ends

In this dull, dead hole.
It's a world all by itself,
Silent only when she's still.
Awake, she's a wolf,

Growling at people
Who dare to enter her home.
One day when she grows feeble,
Box will become tomb.

(Untitled)

My mother taught me
to love, in spite of all the wire
and bombs she tied around herself.

I learned a furious kind of devotion,
bound to the woman who brought me
to the world, yet kept her heart apart
from all who lived there.

When I was young, I didn't know the distance
stretching endless between my mother
and everyone else was a sea she'd built
to make her life a lonely island —
cold and gray, but mostly safe.
She could not give herself away.

My mother wore anger as other women
wear bright colors. Nearly every day,
she painted her self-portrait with exquisite irritation,
ready to make of each hour
another brush stroke in her picture.
That was the mother my childhood remembers.

But the closing chapters also matter.
She quieted, she softened; she lost her
sparring partner — my father.
She gave her soul to waiting,
often patient, though sometimes restless,
until one midnight, finally, following
the path of her last breath,
she escaped.

Demons

What would it take to truly face my demons?

When it began, I didn't mind, not much, because
I needed to be close to someone
as much as he did, and I didn't know,
and maybe he didn't either. I don't know.

But it happened too many times, it hurt,
and the guilt, the dirt, the worthlessness
and ugliness of me, unlovable, trash, my mother
never hugged me, never told me that
she loved me, and what could I do? Crash.

When she found out, when the sins came out,
she said, "It happened to me when I
was fourteen. It's happening all over again,
to her" — that is, to me, her daughter.

What happens happens for so
many reasons, a kind of perfect storm
of bad circumstances, confused emotions
and nowhere to put them except
on the people closest to you.

This is me, I'm spitting it out, sometimes
on the ones now closest to me —
although it's not my husband's fault
he has a man's hands that might
frighten me, not my sons' fault
they were born boys, and when they won't
let me go but jump at me and hold
tightly to me and don't want me to go
and won't won't won't let me go and
goddammit you have to *let me go!*

I hope they can try to understand
when they're older, but now,
heaven help them, they just don't know.

But many times, I love to hug
and hold my beautiful sons,
and tell them I love them every day —
sometimes saying I love them
when I don't know what else to say.
It's hard to comprehend how my mother
could *not* hug her children, when I
cannot *not* hug mine — at least,
most of the time.

When she was fourteen, long long
before she was my mother,
she lost something of herself —
I'm sure of this. And all the years
of no hugs, no love yous, and her anger
the room she lived in, the pleasures
so few and small — and now almost
no pleasures at all, and no hope —
this sad woman, who was a girl
of fourteen, violated by a man she knew,
had ugly demons of her own, demons
more vicious and persistent than mine.
My mother, poor mother,
my sister-survivor, for so very long
I will love you so, even if you have to go.

Underwater Thing

I sat on the floor
and waited for your entrance:
a piece of drama torn
from the water, a weight
leaving me, yet living
in my untaught arms.
I rested when I could,
but restless, impatient as rain.
You took the time you needed,
while I tried to be glad.
You, you are with me
constantly, even more
than your father —
you and I wait together,
we sit on the floor
of the ocean,
all these weary months,
till you step out
and make the world your own.

A Slice of Otto B.

He is friendliest and most vulnerable when he's drunk, or says, "I'm *really* drunk, that's why I can't play these songs,"
On the piano. I am so close I can smell him. I'm kneeling next to his piano player's bench — knees to the floor, left hand on the music machine, the right fisted only an inch from his leg. He
Makes me restless, and I want to ask, "Why do you drink so much, why do you drink every day?"
These are words I do not say.
He says that he plays badly, but I feel he plays for me. So those minutes I was
Thrilled, so thrilled I shook a little more with every interrupted song, every long look he gave so honestly to me that I was too petrified to give back. I did not care when midnight passed us by.
Finally I left him, and he kissed my roommate. I wonder how it tasted, but say I do not care. I tell myself that no kiss matters — even one that
Never happened to me but to someone else — no kiss that comes from a fucking drunk …
Even a fascinating fucking drunk like Phil.

Waterfall

After the concert, we walked away
from my friends and the rest of the crowd
and towards the little bridge
across the water. Holding hands, we walked
down the slope and stepped onto
the bridge, then turned to face
the waterfall upstream. You said
it was a pretty place, and we stood
there, taking in all the green,
the rush of the fall, the shimmering
air of another damp New England day —
wet grass and leaves, wet you and me
with the stream speaking beneath us.
After some few quiet moments, I took
your hand and walked you away
from the bridge, to the Tea Hut
and Paradise Pond, back into the crowds
and to my friends. Your hand is warm,
strong, dry — even dry, somehow, in the rain —
and seems a good match for mine.

Cages

Because I could not hope to hope
Because inside I can't be free, be me

At 2:30 am, the quiet tick, tick,
always sounds like a drip,
dripping in the kitchen, until
I remember the clock.
Tonight, my head's hissing
and fuzzy — I'm sick, the waves
in the dark room move
like lost dogs.

Most days, I want more
or too much from myself.
The clouds surround me
on the ground: pinning my arms,
obstructing the light.
My God! How can they be so tight?

But nighttime gives me
what I expect — stepping soft,
slow, almost silent, it leaves
room for its souls to think.
I can even hear that drip — tick, tick.

I've forgotten what I used to mean,
what I used to dream,
how to lower my stock
of wasted days, how to scream
and fill the empty spaces,
how to pull myself back,
how to lift my heart again
into the sky, with my own hands.

Too long I'm standing still —
more often sitting. Hell,
no wonder I want out of here,
imagine my life is a cage.
But if I could walk enough,
so far enough, maybe
I'll find I guess I might
find me: sitting still,
inside this body, still free,
but waiting to wake.

Apples and Hot Chocolate

Faith has no use for me:
I have the proof, I've seen

a truth, clear as the dog's shadow
under his rusty, disjointed chain.

The sun warms the floor,
my feet, these precious windows.

I believe in skyshine,
a heat on my bed,

and the dream that, finally,
spring has arrived and means

to stay. Apples and hot chocolate
are enough of ecstasy,

tastes of celebration. I have proof,
I am exuberant.

I stop the drip of the kitchen sink;
this makes me indestructible.

Evening dawns pinkly,
joyful against the third floor.

Broken Glass ... Madness

The lamp is doubled
on the smooth, glossy
window pane — divided
by a white, splintery
stick of wood.

Reflected, the wall
shimmers like a pool —
a sea of chlorine
that is silver and still
like a slumbering young man.

Outside, breezes slap
leaves and branches, but grow
softer towards the ground. Now,
darkness has a vise-like grip
on the glass, and won't let up.

The lower half
of the pane is newer.
My anger was the knife
which caused the glass to splinter.
What were my hands thinking of?

Wild

Above this day, the sky
shakes a quiet rage, puts on
its wild dark robe, and starts
to roll a storm across the ground.

In this house, a woman
drops her self, takes up a fake,
and tries to make happy
with other people's recipes.

The sky has countless colors, patterns
of light time and nighttime. Sea waves
push and rush their going and coming.
This is the way I am made:
my colors and form by my own whim,
my will not tuned to anyone
but the constantly shifting rhythm
in the music of the world.

Happier Time

Between the waves and beneath
my heart, I keep you.
Nonsense chatter rattles my head.
I cannot see your face, but know
it is growing —
and every day makes
a little less sense and needs
a little more sleep.
You are the promise I keep:
to bring you to the outside
whole and wailing, to see
you clothed, growing, fed,
to believe a happier time's
not far ahead.

Electrical Storm

Lightning splits the sky,
straight up from the trees.
Only moments later,
night has closed over
the wound, sealing
it without a scar.

A bolt tears my body in two:
Sure, I'm as lucky
as you, and you.
Perhaps I am healing
slowly, still becoming whole.

I am not the sky, but my heart
looks something like it:
wide open,
a constant motion,
a crowding round this world.

The Walk
(for Rolin)

It's April. Winter
grips the woods.

The forest path cries
under ice.

We stroll near
a stream, feet slipping

in old snow. I hear
the chilly day

in our breath,
and an echo of highway

by another water body
one hundred miles away.

I forget the year I'm in,
think of Providence, a park

on a dock, filthy water
slapping stones

along the land's edge,
a power plant across the lake.

His voice stops me; we pause
where the walk bends.

He sings a birdcall, listens
to cooing replies. A motor

squawks far off, and he tells
me the world is ending.

I kick a broken branch
off the footpath, but he

smiles, moves it back,
teases, then leaves me.

The water sways my head,
clouds darken the afternoon,

my hands pray for
something warmer than rivers.

A bird repeats my scream.
Day waits. I'm under.

Romance

The beach
was beautiful, you tell me,
shooting off reflections
of stars into the dark
and into his eyes.
But all shores
are special at three in the night —
no exceptions.

Surroundings fade
back into vacuums,
confused as clocks.
As two, you
command the attention of the air
you share, strolling the canal
of your precious mouths.

A quietness ensues,
the waves drop back, and pairs
of lips are parted.
Smiles are caught in sand.
I want to tell you
the music of affection
was not a seaside silence,
but only some damn violins.

Your story is too lovely:
I nod, peeling a tiny smile
from the fake sack, keeping
my lemon mouth tight shut.

Snow Shovels

The snow shovels come out
every day now, just about,
my father clearing the steps
at odd hours, often when
it's still thick and heavy
darkness snowing outside.
He'll shovel three and four times
during a single storm,
maybe he'll sleep in the chair.
Once a shovel slid down
the cellar stairs to where I sat,
a slip scrape wet hitting my back,
a shovel carelessly placed
by my father. I wasn't hurt,
but he worried so — only
a little mishap, nothing.
Still, winter
is what I fear most when
I'm in it: shivering
even in my day sleep,
viewing the house through ice,
believing shovels could cut
anything, and dreaming (almost
not breathing) of the day
when their metal remembers this.

Losing Everything but Our Appetites

(for William Henry McCarty Burke, Sept. 12, 1941 – May 8, 2005)

June 29, 2005

I went for a walk last evening, and listened to some of Patty Griffin's *1000 Kisses* while I walked. I saw an airplane flying low over my head, and kept looking up, then back behind me, as I walked, to watch it fly away. A few minutes later, there it was again, circling, and I watched it once more, still flying low, and I was still walking and listening to Patty. My two little boys love to see airplanes, especially the ones cruising low in our neighborhood. Since we only live a few miles from Forbes Field, we see them fairly often. I had felt on the verge of tears all day, and exhausted, thinking of all the things I still needed to deal with, these weeks after my father's death. The third time the plane went over, I started thinking about how Kyle and Ryan would never get to show their Grandpa Burke, my Daddy, the big planes that regularly fly low over their house, and circle around their neighborhood. The fourth time the plane went over, I had reached the front of our house, my husband and sons inside, me crying, Patty singing — though no one could hear her but me — and I went up the front steps, sat down by the front door, and sobbed. It was one of the few times I really needed a tissue in my pocket, and it figures I didn't have one. I went inside, blew my nose, and slipped back into my real life.

{w.h.b.}

The night after the day after my father died, I didn't sleep very well. I woke up soon after midnight, thinking of him, remembering what he was like when I was little. I started crying, and after a few minutes, I left Ryan, my littlest boy, and went down to the living room. I didn't try to read, didn't do any writing, didn't turn on the TV, only sat on the sofa, in the light of a small lamp, and thought of Da, and cried.

After half an hour, or forty-five minutes, I went back to bed, eventually went back to sleep. But I was up again before morning came, and by the time the sun crept up, Jeff was in the kitchen with me, and I told him about my Daddy.

{w.h.b.}

I had always wanted a normal dad, but if I'd had him, he wouldn't have been Daddy. My father was a very big man, and proud of it: six-foot-five, size thirteen shoes, well over 200 pounds, and steadily heavier as the years passed. In his last years, he had reached 300. He loved food, and had an appetite like no one else I've ever known. My Aunt Helen told me a story once about Da, that at Thanksgiving, when he was a teenager, Daddy would eat turkey continuously, until finally Grandma Burke would tell him he had to stop because the meal was over and the family was moving on to dessert. My father himself told me once — or twice — that he'd always considered pizza more a snack than a meal. He said he could eat a whole pizza himself after being out in the afternoon, and still eat dinner when he got home. I remember the four of us — Mommy, Daddy, Lee, and me — eating lunch at Kentucky Fried Chicken once when I was young, maybe seven or eight years old. Daddy was finishing up the pieces Lee and I had started eating and then rejected. If there was any meat left, my father ate it. My mother started telling him to stop eating, and before long I was repeating her, becoming more convinced with every bite that my father would soon explode with chicken.

Da was hit by a car on September 20, 2004, but even though the car ran over his legs, it had been going slowly and my father was not admitted to the hospital. During his time in the emergency room that day, Da was hungry enough that he walked down to the cafeteria, ate, and walked back. He said that walk back was especially painful, and at that point he did get in a wheelchair. That's my dad, putting the needs of his stomach above everything else, and forgetting his common sense. (I don't believe that accident, months earlier, was related to his passing in any way. It took some time for his legs to recover, but from what he had told me, I think his legs had healed to be about as good as they were before it happened.)

{w.h.b.}

In the eight or nine months before Da died, I had been on a diet and exercise program and had lost 30 pounds. In the seven weeks or so since his death, I find it harder and harder to eat well, to exercise, to resist the temptations of my favorite meals, snacks, and fattening drinks. The first few times after Da's death that I went to the café in Hastings to get my usual drink, the wonderfully sweet chocolate coffee ice cube blender concoction known as the Heath Mocha Frost, I'd look around while the café employee made my drink, and my eyes would tear up, as I thought of my dad. To me, the Heath Mocha Frost is more than just a wonderful cold beverage. It represents a lot of other things: fun stuff I'd like to buy but can't afford, things I'd like to do but never have enough time, and perhaps it even reminds me of people I used to know and care about that I've lost touch with. The café in Hastings has become so familiar to me the past few years, that it's not only the center of my favorite store, but a place where my heart can breathe and rest. And a couple of weeks after Da died, I actually did start crying as soon as I got out of the store with my drink, and sat in my car alone for five minutes, letting out some of the sadness that had built up in my mind. I fully believe that my recent increase in eating is connected with my grief, though I can't exactly say how. I get my appetite from my father, while the need to clear my plate whenever possible, I attribute to a childhood where food was not always plentiful. I'm driven toward my delectable chocolate coffee drinks to give me some peace and contentment, to comfort me, as my father cannot comfort me now, he is gone.

{w.h.b.}

Eating as he did, my father had a big belly — which might have been called a beer belly, though he rarely drank alcohol. The morning after the night I couldn't sleep, I remembered his belly, hugging him when I was a teenager (one of the rare moments of closeness during my stormy adolescence), and how when I was young, I could rest my head on his belly — him on the sofa watching television, and me lying across, and using his stomach as a pillow. A little girl could not have felt safer than I felt, with the sense that I was just where I belonged. I told Jeff on that Tuesday morning, He was my Daddy, I was his little girl. However strange and crazy the world turned out to be, in those years to come, I had always been his little girl. I still remember walking down the street with him, my big tall Daddy who I could hide behind, he holding my hand, and I holding two of his fingers. I tend to walk fast, to this day, and I'm sure the behavior is rooted in those early years — walking with my father, moving my little legs along to keep up with him, as he held my hand.

When I was about eleven years old, and we lived in the building next to County Square, there was a full lunar eclipse. It was summertime. I had wanted to see the eclipse, but my mother didn't want me to — the height of it was in the middle of the night. My father's sleeping patterns had always been somewhat erratic: he could fall asleep almost anywhere, and yet would also sleep through an alarm that could wake me up in the next room. He thought nothing of getting up at 4 am to have his morning coffee and do whatever he felt like doing, and then napping on the bed in the afternoon while the television blared away. The night of the eclipse, when I woke up, my father was up and outside, and I went out to join him — probably between 3 and 4 am. We walked around County Square, before the morning traffic, looking at the sky. We went down to Morin's Diner, where Daddy worked, and had breakfast around 5 or 5:30 am.

Thinking about it now, I see that when I was little, my relationship with my father was often like that: whatever he was doing, there was room for me to join him — if not in the activity, at least on the sidelines. I was welcomed in his world, and my brother was, too. We both would watch him play softball with some of his friends on Sundays after church. He took us swimming at the public pool across town — which sometimes meant hitchhiking, since our smaller feet got sore along the way. I wouldn't dream of hitchhiking now, even with another person, but with Daddy, it was never scary, it was exciting, and we loved getting a ride. Da even took us to the beach near Boston — the train from Attleboro to South Station, the subway out to Revere, stopping at Wonderland, by the greyhound race track, because we found out there were shower facilities there. I remember him lying on the bed, propped up on his left arm, working on the checkbook — I watched him printing, mostly in caps, writing out checks and updating the register, doing one of those mysterious and important grown-up things — and I learned the basics of how to write checks and keep the register up to date. I've had a checking account continuously since I turned eighteen, and I'm proud of my role as keeper of the checkbook and payer of the bills for our family of four.

{w.h.b.}

July 30, 2005

Today is Saturday, and my birthday; I am 34. I went for my long walk this morning, to get my Heath Mocha Frost, and I pushed Ryan in the stroller for the first half of the journey — more vigorous exercise than merely walking. It was a very good walk, not nearly as hot as the last two Saturdays, and Ryan was cooperative, and we enjoyed each other's company. It was a good way to start a birthday, and to end a tiresome week. Life is always so hectic, and my mind grows ever more fractured. When there is so much to do, where do I start?

How can I focus on anything, when there are dozens of other thoughts and duties crowded on the edge of my vision?

A few weeks ago, my brother sent me my father's high school yearbook. I recalled that there was writing in it, but I didn't realize before, or perhaps I just didn't remember, that most of the writing in it was done by my father. I think of yearbooks as things that other people write in for you, and you write in theirs — but my father's is different. Reading it, I could imagine him writing away in it, whatever he was thinking, in the same way that he couldn't be quieted when he was manic — he just talked on and on, whatever came through his head. The writings in the yearbook sounded in my ear the same way. There is small evidence for this idea. My father occasionally wrote letters to various relatives, in those wee hours when he was up drinking his Sanka and the rest of us were still sleeping. He wrote those letters with greater frequency when he was manic. In the years after I went away to grad school and then got married, I received a few of those letters, where thoughts were noted as they came to him, whether or not they followed logically from the previous sentence.

I wonder, as lately my own mind scatters beyond my ability to hold on to it, did my father ever have this kind of problem? Is this just what happens when you have a demanding full-time job, an equally busy spouse and two ornery kids at home, cleaning to do in said home, shopping, paying bills, and everything else pulling at your attention? I've never been manic, but I wonder if there's some connection between a brain spinning in overdrive, as his was at those times, and another that's overwhelmed and can't zero in on the task at hand, as mine is these days.

When I looked at the picture of my father in his yearbook — a picture I've seen many times — I saw what he'd noted as his ambition: "To be successful in everything I undertake." He was young, good-looking (yes, even THIN back then!), intelligent, good-humored, and came from a good home. He was friendly, confident — and had been the comic lead in the high school play (he'd told me many times). Did he ever think of that statement, and compare it with his life? How did he define "successful"? Did he even mean it, when he put it in there, or was it another joke from the comic lead? I cannot ask him these questions. If we hold up the usual definition of "successful" against my dad, most would agree he was not, and would say he was far from it. I believe that, too, which is hard to admit.

But I know this: my father was a good man. He was as good a husband and father as he could be, and took good care of us — he was a gentle giant. He was a very hard worker, and dedicated; after he first lost his job at Morin's in the 1990s, he wanted nothing more than steady employment, a steady paycheck. Da was often friendly, and maintained his sense of humor all through his difficult life. I found it hard to list his interests and hobbies, when providing information for his obituary. As I asked the priest who later performed the graveside service, "How can you say, 'There was nothing he liked more than a good laugh'?" That was true about him — though sometimes a laugh or joke was tied for first with a good meal. Had he been successful? Probably not as he once hoped to be. But he and my mother raised me. I always wished for "normal" parents, a "normal" family, and yet I would not be myself if not for them.

I remember asking my Aunts Helen and Anne, when I was about 17, if they thought I looked like either of them. One of them said — and I don't know which one — "Actually, I see a lot of Harry in you." Unforgettable words for a teenage girl, a young woman ... God forbid! But there is a lot to be proud of, too. He was a good person. Perhaps I can be a good person, too.

{w.h.b.}

Earlier this week, I received my second letter from a company which provides a safety net for credit card debt. I hadn't read the first letter closely, and thus had not acted upon it. But after receiving the second letter, which was requesting a copy of Da's death certificate, I called them to find out more. It turns out that when my father applied for his First Premier Bank credit card, he also signed up for that protection where — as I told the man on the phone — "if you lose your job, or your leg, or if you die," the company will pay off your debt on that card. I verified with the man that this protection was one of those things where they charge a monthly fee on your card; it was something like 68 cents for each $100.00 balance on the card. I was incredulous — MY FATHER had actually paid EXTRA for something??? I said to the man, "It's just very strange to me that my father would have signed up to pay more — he was just never like that at all." After a bit of my carrying on, he said, "Well, I'm glad you can have a sense of humor about it." It wasn't really humor, it was more like disbelief — though I couldn't explain that to him, because what would I say? "It's just that my father was always pretty cheap." No, it wouldn't do.

Perhaps I shouldn't be too surprised, knowing that he did have some credit card debt, and some other small debts, when he passed away, and knowing too, because I now get his mail, that he had subscribed to such magazines as *Gourmet*, *Better Homes & Gardens*, *Men's Journal*, *Entrepreneur*, *Field and Stream* — all manner of things that he didn't need. As my Aunt Helen said in those first days after my dad died, "Harry was always a magazine guy." I have no doubt that he found some of those topics interesting to read about, but there was nothing in them that reflected his daily life. Of course he subscribed to *TV Guide*, *Sports Illustrated*, *Time*, and *ESPN, The Magazine* — those are old stand-bys — but *Entrepreneur*? When he was a younger man, my father had excellent credit, and was rightly proud of that fact: he paid his bills on time,

and generally paid his debts off early. My guess is that, after years of only intermittent employment, receiving Social Security each month felt a bit like winning a prize, bringing with it a sense of relief, and something to rely on, but also greater freedom to spend a little more than he probably should have. And we're a nation of consumers, after all — so many of us, myself included, trying to fill the empty pieces of ourselves with more <u>stuff</u> — or with more food, see above.
{w.h.b.}

However unfortunate and premature my father's death, I have found some consolation in the fact that he did not suffer when he passed on. Isn't it what so many people hope for, to die peacefully during sleep? He didn't have a terminal illness, like cancer, that would have brought great pain, and likely a slow decline. He wasn't in and out of the hospital over the course of months or years, as my Grandpa Allen was, and so many others who were regulars at Sturdy Memorial Hospital, where I worked for eight years. He hadn't been in a car accident or suffered a traumatic fall. The way I think of it is, he simply bowed out. He'd had a taste of illness, of hospitalization, in March, and by his fifth day there, he was itching to get out. He didn't want to have a doctor and nurse's permission to use the bathroom or do anything else, and he was bored of the place. Rather than go through a long decline, clinging to life at any cost, his soul and body had a chat and decided, "No thanks, we don't want to do that," and while my father slept on his bed — a place where he had enjoyed endless hours of TV programs, joined in the excitement when one of his teams was playing well, read his magazines, smoked cigarettes, ate almost daily, listened to hundreds of his beloved records, and sometimes paid his bills, and where my mother slept too, before she was moved permanently to the nursing home — his body stilled, and his soul slipped away in the darkness.

The End of the Story for the Lover of Books

*I am not a literary critic; I am a Lover of Books, and of their
    Endless Kisses.*

I am thinking of peacefulness.
Me, lying down, wrapped tight and safe
in the pages of books. No skin shows
through the thousands of leaves, the hundreds
of hard and soft covers. There are novels
and poems, of course, and occasional
essays, but also, of late, more books
about books, about reading and writers,
each volume containing dozens more,
and these are the softest parts of the quilt.

When I cannot read them — no solitary time,
too little ambition — they still comfort me,
enclosed in a cloud, or at rest in a shroud
where I hear only the rustle of paper
and the murmur of words, some written
centuries past. They demand nothing
from me, and give me release,
a moment of peace — from pain,
and from my heavy heart
in the world of the living.

Me, My Dad, and Patty Griffin

I walked with Patty singing in my ears,
her music flowing freely as the creek
beside the trail. My head had been too full,
splitting all week — an out-of-town meeting
the past three days. On Saturday, all that
got mixed with Patty's *Impossible Dream*
and remembering, missing my father.

Always, it seems, we try to justify
our very selves, the space we occupy.
Sometimes, I am so tired of fighting life.
When will what I do be enough, and when,
when will it be done? The tears sprinkled
my cheeks with grief, my soul with
something like comfort, my head with relief.

In tangled thoughts, I pushed myself so hard
along the trail that I felt Patty's voice
filling my body, refreshing the empty well,
and acting as a compass I could follow
through all my changing moods and days,
the peaceful, yellow, angry, sweet, or gray.
Her words return me to my self.

It's been almost six months, and sometimes I
still catch myself thinking I'll call Da
and tell him that - - - but then I remember
I can't. One quiet Saturday, I emptied out
my eyes, trying to find my balance, and
I let Patty's songs fill me up again.
But still, if I call my parents' old number,
I'll only reach my brother.
More than my father himself, and his life,
I miss the sound of his voice on the line,
the phone like an anchor I can never pull up again.

Schism

I never dreamed this sea:
she sits, rolling her eyes
at me because I

won't swim, but only
watch her turning inside
herself, around a sane

and ageless heart. Her dance
is safe and steady —
wet legs stretching toward land,

gray fingers spraying ships.
Like a photo, some scene
from any scrapbook:

white waves are almost
breaking, the sand sparkles,
everywhere reflects stars.

You know how the moon looks,
colder than romance.
And me, I'm in this room

sweating as if summer
were living in my skin,
and lonely kicks me

before I can stand.
The water takes the sand.
I can't get out the door.

Asylum

The walls are white — frozen ice — the years
I've been here — waiting, wishing to escape.
My arms and legs are bound; I am long, hard,
stiffly straight: a wooden telephone pole.
I choke on a cloth damp with saliva,
and sweat, as it pours from my skin.

The walls are black — sticky tar — the years
I've been here — chained and glued to the corner.
My face is inhuman, immersed
in dust and cobwebs, with skin chipping off.
I am lost, sliced away from reality, unable to see
past my window, and its steel bars.

The walls are red — my own blood — the years
I've been here; my soul is burned away,
its ashes a gift for you. I can still see the green
of the oaks, and taste the ocean's salt;
they linger outside the heart's walls.
There, outside the asylum, freedom waits for me.

A Little Piece

My dirty boots coming through the door
to a house all silent, deserted, and I
am still searching, weary.

I wonder at the sweetheart man
I married, our pretty infant son,
and I wonder where I came from.

Sometimes I think my soul has gone
to sleep, afraid to see
what happened to my life:

such a bright and shiny skin,
but hard for me to move in.
I can't help guessing, some days,

who I might be, if I were free.

Snow Day

Our insecurities
are showing, dear.
We're standing in a field
with hush-white walls
binding my stars to yours,
and me, feeling
penned, not moving an inch.
The sky hangs low.
You back away, your face
makes its own speech:
"I'm gone, I can't love you."
Your mouth sticks shut.
The field has a fever,
the air is still,
a forest recedes like
water, my ears
are screaming — Do you hear?
Can you? — and walls
do not protect, my arms
flying crazy;
all rivers run cold on
this barren ground.
No mountain can hold me.
Love cracks. Silence.

Baptism

The water is a beginning, I suppose,
and an escape.
This is called walking out.
My legs are heavy,
and slow, slowly,

the sea inches up and becomes more.
Waves are humanity turning over,
what I go for and long
to be a part of.
My hips are so cold.

Depth is inconceivable;
it seems a far space off,
yet even my hair and
face in the water
seem too deep for me.

Alone, I step into the ocean,
carrying an idea that I will not come
back, ever. I am settled,
becoming a worm to the water,
more sand for the bottom.

One Thousand Thousand

What would happen if one woman told the truth about her life?
The world would split open
　　　　　　--- from "Käthe Kollwitz" by Muriel Rukeyser

1.
There is someone for everyone, they say.
I am someone for everyone — someone
different for almost everyone I know.
I ponder this while pushing my littlest son
in his swing, the afternoon before
a storm threatens but never lands here.
Of course I'm exhausted, completely spent
like last week's paycheck. It's hard
to be someone for everyone else.
I steal my alone moments whenever I can
and find myself defensive when I'm caught.

2.
My first trip home from grad school
took me about sixteen hours.
I woke in Tucson, loaded myself down
with bags, took two buses to the airport,
changed planes in Dallas (with no time
to spare — I sat by two teenage boys,
we were all three reading Dean Koontz),
landed in Boston, took three subways
to South Station, and waited
for the local to take me home.
While I waited, an old man told me,
"You must have broken someone's heart,
at least once." I confessed, yes.
I read my book, ate, and rested.
When I got off the train, I called
a taxi, then my parents to say

I'd made it. In fifteen minutes,
I, my bags, and sore shoulders were home.

3.
As I returned Smiley's *A Thousand Acres*,
in tears I told my aunt — I told her,
"I was sexually abused as a child."
She said through her own tears,
"You've really lived a thousand lives,
haven't you?" I told her, "Yes.
Yes, I have." And now
it's ten years later. I've lost count.

4.
One young man, way back when.
His face was rough with stubble.
I said I thought we should stop.
At first I thought he would.
Then he turned me over,
laid on my back, and I saw
the headboard in the darkness,
and knew I was letting God down.
Down.
Down.
Faraway.
Drown.

5.
With my older son, labor pains
lasted all weekend, starting late
Friday night, and finally ending
with a Cesarean section at 3:29
on Monday morning. Valentine's Day.
More morphine, please.
My younger son was a scheduled
repeat section, in some ways easier.
Still, I remember how the spinal

numbed even my lungs — like iron
binding my chest for endless seconds.
My only movement was turning my head,
while Jeff, bless him, held the basin,
and I vomited nine months of waiting
and one vile-tasting medication.
Then I was a mother of two.

6.
November, frigid wind.
As darkness swells, my perspective
shrinks to a world only
the size of a fallen branch,
the color of a rotten pumpkin.
I would not be amazed if my veins
burst open on their own, splitting
skin quick as ripping paper.
All the pressures of everyday
building like clouds, and me
buried underneath.
The old little girl hurts linger.
Then I remind myself to breathe,
and think tonight might be better.
Yes, it might.

7.
So many women live a thousand lives.
In one of mine, I'm hoping you
are just around every corner I turn.
I am constantly seeking your face,
the wondrous spirit I see
in the light of your eyes.
Sometimes when I'm alone, I silently
mourn the stories I'll never tell
to you — beautiful you, never mine.
But still, that's only in one
of my thousands of lives.

Tank

Clean water, my body
into your body,
an aura of immortality.
Light strikes
and bends across our parts.

The pool is deep,
a bouquet of fish —
such colors and mouths!
Most are smooth, dull as rubber
and no threat to me.

Some mouths touch,
some rip and cut.
The creatures swim round
and round me like so many
satellites, shimmering

in their own
loud garden.
What a bed this is,
what a way to live along —
heated, nearly natural.

Wet fish come close,
scenting through their gills,
a floating mass of plastic eyes.
We are lips
on lips, these fish and I,

in a basin large enough
for all of us.
We move in communion.
Legless, I am a ship
of skin and boards.

Corner Story

In a shadowed corner
my lunatic legs
are embracing a chair
hot as black steel,
and I'm bleeding.

The air falls down.
Such cruel blooms spill
out of my mouth,
surrounding my toes.
The infection grows.

All sounds are outside
my ears, echoes
from stone in between.
I cannot know more,
it won't hold in here.

I am alone in the corner.
I am my own tormentor.
This is a rope, this is a whip;
red anger's the death slip
I hang myself with.

The Breaking

I knew it, too, I knew before
you said it's gotten too
too hard for you, and then
you said you were not sure
if it should be the breaking end.
I didn't press too hard — I knew
you felt more terrible than
your every word was to me.

The sun could not decide to stay
in or out, it flew across my bed
and then behind the clouds. Noon
brought scurrying raindrops.
The wind was warmer
than before, the leaves more dead
now. I knew today would be
so blue, I chose clothes only blue.
Earrings, necklace, my two
green eyes with tears on top,
your jacket — these were all blue, too.
The sky was bland and gray,
its water washed you away.

Children's Television

I was eight, I think,
or nine, when I
slept on the sofa
in the living room.
I don't remember the reason.

I remember my mother
watched *Helter Skelter*
when I was curled up there,
waiting for sleep, listening.
I learned that Susan Atkins

had tasted a victim's blood.
I heard the prosecutor
(an actor) speaking
the roll call of the dead,
names shivering in air.

My mother also owned
the book, with those
ghastly photos
in the middle: each body
positioned as it

had been left, and found,
but rubbed white,
erased from the picture.
The six hundred pages
bloodied the blank spots.

I hated knowing
that this book, its empty
ghostly photos,
sat on our bookshelf.
It frightened me for years —

as if it were murder,
the crime itself, its words
in blood on my walls.
I hid it on the bottom
shelf, tried to forget.

I was thirteen, yes,
when I read it — twice.
At sixteen, I bought my own copy.
The roll call continues
today, in my head,

and I know those names
like a bit of my skin
and I have never been
to California, but I slept there
in some previous life.

Universal Event

What I have discovered:
the heat will kill us all.
Do what you wish, while you can.

Some days the days
are unemotional:
no one feels it, not at all.

The greens are clearly stale
and dull. The clouds are slack,
they go nowhere.

Even sleep
is no escape:
dreams are strangers here.

It used to be beautiful —
I walked about smiling.
The trees envied me my motion.

I breathe a silent
and unhappy air;
we share our common paralysis.

This is a global event.
The world is done to death,
and I can't …

(Tick. Tick. Tick.)

One Evening

Solitary, stone eyes
blank, passionless,
young woman
pushes herself,
needs no one.
Face dark with
exhaustion, it is worn
older than its years.

Man, a tornado,
wrecks woman's stability,
strips her strength, beats her
into herself. Safety
returns her to her kind,
while his presence
marks each gesture,
every mood.
Passing the house where
her flesh was ravished,
she can't discern it
in the daytime.

A Family's Fences

The years pile up, link
together the wants
and defeats
of one and two people,
or three, who think
that being family
is all you need to love.

The roof is leaking,
walls fall off slowly,
and the fence
cannot build itself.
A family cuts its own ties
with its bare teeth.
All leave the yard bleeding.

You cannot forget this:
after all the reaching
toward a television harmony,
death will rush up
and take you on the left.
No fence will be so honest,
then, as your memory,

dressed in blue, waving to you.

My Home

Home? It is cotton-soft,
the warm amid the coolest air.
It is a human chair;
my body rests on his.

Yes, this is the place
that made me so curious:
held to his chest
in mutual trust,
head on my arm,

cool hand on his neck,
sometimes cheek to cheek.
I seem at home
in his soothing arms,
I regress to the womb.

Oh why
are you not my mother?
I might leave my body,
return to her,
cease to be, to remember

myself. Here, your arms and legs
are a wrapping paper
wonderful and wide
as the night sky.

I want to shut my eyes.
You take me closer,
then fear tightens my throat.
Your hand moves near my heart.
You almost had me there.

Redcoat Lane

Down Redcoat Lane, I found
a sweet and sunny hive.
I found a man living inside —
chinless, soft-eyed, drinking
hard drinks every night.

I was prepared to hate him.
The door opened and spoke
my name — a juice from the hinges,
juice in a ferment beneath
a full moon. He took me

on an upstairs tour,
he took me to his room.
The fish tank was warm, my face
the same, and my feelings changed
beside the bookcase — a seduction

played out, neat as the shelves.
We stared a moment, shared
words that floated on their own.
I wish I had kissed him
in the street: lit by lamps

and a round yellow moon.
He held me in my fantasy —
I mean, there in the street.
Redcoat Lane is a place
where I got lost, once.

An Attempt at Prayer

Without hands,
how can I claw my way
up out of a scorched hole?
It is so dirty here,
where I hate myself most
of all. Nothing shines inside this.

Tonight, I wanted
to pray. Seeing holy statues
in blackness, sitting
in a dark chapel
without a Mass happening,
dropping a flaming match
onto a candle of my best
intentions …
all I could do was weep.
I ended this prayer with "Amen."

Perhaps I have forgotten
what prayer means,
and how to do it.
Though now, I realize that
perhaps I have never known
how to do it.

Can such a thing be taught
to me, or to anyone?
I must learn
to believe in my nighttime.
Then, my hands might grow,
proper and new, knowing
how to fold themselves
in a quiet humility,
learning to grasp the walls

of this gray human cell,
the depths of hell
in my mind, in what I am.

Rocks and a Newport Shore

I'm haunted
by the sound of drowning pebbles
dropped onto the shore,
pulled to water's edge.
It comes after sleep,
and half-waking, part
of a story I told once.
I remember.

I saw a white line
standing up on the horizon,
stiff string surrounded by blue paper,
crawling away, growing
smaller. The water
waves hello to me before its smile
fades to blankness.

You stop for rocks,
skip stones across the wet.
We sit, not close enough
together, on the shore.
Your words crack the dam,
touch me like fingers
on my face;
your voice

softly squeezes my heart.
I want to kiss you,
make a romantic memory,
but the blueness distracts
me, confuses me.
I cry instead, salt drops
locked in my head.
We set them free.

The sound of Newport
pebbles
hitting each other
on a sunny Sunday
at April's end
goes through my soul
like your tongue when you
kiss me.

A Breath Returning

The sea's edge. Water
flows over my ankles,
consumes my legs,
hands, knees …
and then leaves.

Here, there are
too many rocks
beneath the small waves,
thick weeds keeping
me immobile,

pinned in.
The wet surface
breaks under sun —
a shattering brilliance,
precious as pearls.

Its fury astounds me.
I back away, toward shore,
watching the wild sea
spreading like lips,
into forever.

No Sunrise

I want to be in the sea.
I feel closer to water
than to your family;
the ocean is more like home,
and the camper frightens me.
I should not be here,
I'll never come here,
I didn't know what to wear.

Supper was the hardest part.
You fed me and fed me
but you couldn't see
me needing you.
I didn't offer
to help your mother —
the thought was there,
but sound died in my mouth.

And I cried on the shore,
the edge of the world —
a girl thick in the mist
of an unsleeping sea,
weeping from my own soul,
bleeding from wounds
that are nowhere … but sore.
No sunrise here anymore.

Road Blocks

There's another summer coming, I should
be glowing. Instead, I'm watching

you watching TV, working all day with
less than half my brain, feeling senseless.

I'm standing on a rainbow at night, walking
the line of my life, but wishing it were

a circle, not a jagged ax of road
that points all over, and nowhere.

I step outside, and even the breeze
can hardly touch me. I wonder

why we never play anymore, but only
pass each other in the kitchen

and take turns soothing the baby.
But oh, my little son! If I could just

let him teach me, as he finds his smile
and his hands, that life is not really

a street or a highway. It has far more
detours, its own strange rules, and no map.

Notes on the Poems

"Break of Dawn" was written in late November, probably in 1998, to include with our Christmas cards that year. I always say that November is my worst month, and that it lasts from about October 20 to December 15. In the poem, I'm trying to pull myself out of the doldrums and look toward a brighter future, or at least to being out of November.

"Watching from a Darkened House" and "Cast Party" were both inspired by the time spent with a group of friends as they prepared for the high school play. Most of my close friends were in Drama, all acting, singing, and dancing. I was the happy observer who often wished to be invisible.

"Beavertail" recounts an evening near the seashore, at Beavertail State Park in Rhode Island.

"Newport" was written after I'd read the sonnets of Edna St. Vincent Millay. I caught the rhyme schemes, but hadn't learned about iambic pentameter, so my attempt has an acceptable sonnet rhyme, but the lines aren't quite long enough and don't have the correct "feet." I still like the rhythm of it.

"A Box, a Life" might be the oldest poem in the collection. I've unofficially paired it with the untitled poem that follows it.

"Underwater Thing" was written during my first pregnancy. The title was inspired by the song "Liquid Diamonds" by Tori Amos.

"Asylum" and "Corner Story" were inspired by real emotions, but **not** by real events.

"Tank" was written after a trip to the New England Aquarium in Boston with my then-boyfriend.

"Universal Event" probably sounds like it's about global warming or climate change, but it's another old one, and those phrases weren't in the mainstream media when I wrote it. I believe I wrote it during a summer heatwave, and my parents' apartment didn't have air conditioning. Apologies for the mundane back story.

"A Family's Fences" was written for an American Theater class I took in college. It was inspired by the incredible play by August Wilson called *Fences*. (Put that on your reading list if you aren't familiar with it.)

In case you're wondering, What is the deal with all the imagery of drowning?
Growing up in Massachusetts, very close to Rhode Island (nicknamed the Ocean State), I saw a lot of beaches throughout my childhood and early 20s. I love the beach, and I'm awed by the ocean, but I've never learned to properly swim, and I've always been afraid of dunking my head in the water. (I'm also slightly vain about my hair, so that's the other reason I try not to get too wet above my shoulders.) Something as beautiful, majestic, overwhelming, and frightening as the sea would naturally find its way into a lot of my poems. Clearly, my struggles with depression and thoughts of suicide are also reflected in many of my poems. Having a fascination with both water and death, especially during my stormy adolescence, led me to include a threat of drowning in much of my poetry. Although I'm as far from the ocean now as I can possibly be, I still feel inspired by it.

Acknowledgments

Because this is my first published book, and because a few of these poems were written as far back as the late 1980s, I feel a need to thank almost everyone I've ever met. I will try to resist that urge.

First, thank **you**, dear reader, for taking a chance on my book! I hope you enjoyed it.

Ma and Da, who loved me more than they were able to express, cared for me as well as they could, and had faith that my mind might take me to a better place if I worked hard enough. They were right. I miss them both.

Jeff, Kyle, and Ryan, for all the good things you do, and for loving me in spite of myself.

Sue, for being an excellent mom, mom-in-law, and Grandma — taking care of everyone, feeding and sitting for the kids all these years, and being probably the best cook I've ever known. I cannot thank you enough.

Stacy and Rick, Justin and Lisa — thanks for accepting this East Coast girl into your family.

My Aunt Helen, and my friend Pat P. (still the Best Boss Ever!), two strong and wonderful women who both told me I was smart enough to go to a "real" four-year college, away from home. I don't know how far I would have gotten without that encouragement from both of you, at just the right time. Thank you thank you, a hundred times over.

My cousin Valerie and her family (who always open their home to me when I'm in their neck of the woods), as well as my cousin Heidi and Aunt Barbara. Thank you especially for the kindness you always showed to my mom, and continue to show by visiting my parents' grave when you can. It means a great deal to me.

I named Aunt Helen above, but all of my aunts and uncles on my father's side have given me huge amounts of love and support. Uncle Jim, Aunt Anne and Uncle Richard, and Uncle Tom: I aspire to be more like all of you.

Marie P-J, my oldest friend. I wish we lived closer to one another. You are always in my thoughts and in my heart.

Friends from middle and high school who encouraged (and often endured!) my poetic efforts, and continue to do so: Janna, Jules, Denise, Melissa S., Gina, Karl, and Leigh Ann. Shout out to the high school friends with whom I shared the "Fab Five" summers and New Year's Eves: Heather, Debbie D., Brian, and Tom S. I lost so much sleep because of you guys, but I wouldn't trade a minute!

Debbie F. — I didn't know when we worked together at the hospital, so many years ago, that you'd be my friend forever. Lucky for me, you're one of the kindest and most loving people in the world. Thank you for being you, Deb!

All my Smith friends, both from Sessions and from the *Grecourt Review*, and I'm sorry if I'm forgetting people: Kirsten (my Big Sister!), Lori, Sarah, Anne Marie, Amy B. (now Amy H.), Leslie F., Fiona, Valerie C., Kerry, Morgan, Susie, Meghan L., Dia, Megan G., and in memory of Miriam, who left us too early. Also, in a class by herself, Elizabeth B. (There's a hole in this bucket, Dear Liza, Dear Liza. I still miss you.)

My favorite Smith professors, who inspired me to work harder: Robert Hosmer, Doug Patey, William Oram, Patricia Miller (who told the best stories in Intro Sociology), and Howard Adelman.

Jennifer, whom I met at CCRI, and stayed with when I first moved to Tucson. I miss you, but it makes me so happy that you're managing a bookstore now — yay!

Speaking of Tucson, I made some wonderful friends at University of Arizona. Thank you to Gwen A., Julie H., Christa G., Lynnette B., Ben and Lisa, Mary B., and Kathy H., who hosted my wedding reception at her home! Special thanks to Charley, my favorite U. of A. professor, who also became a great friend.

Finally, I'm grateful for the friendship and support of my local pals and co-workers, especially: all of Jeff's extended family, who made me feel welcome from day one; all of the McLaughlin friends, who did the same; Lynn W-K, Penny D., Becky W., Stephanie C., Audrey, Jacob G., Lissa, Miranda; and the sports and school parents, in particular: Sheila and Bobby, Julie and Steve, Dana and Travis, Kim and Chad, Nikki and John, Carrie and Scott, Bridget and Kelly, Margaret, Katrina, Brad, Robyn and Bob, and Craig.

All the members of the James Joyce Lemonade Society book club, including Barbara L., Leslie G., Marilyn S., David B., Roy L., Gwen S., Marge A., Bob W. and Maria S.; and in memory of Bob L., Jim A., and Gail H. My book group were some of my first friends in Kansas, and they practically adopted me. Thank you for all the years of friendship and fantastic reading!

My transportation colleagues around the country, including: Maggie and Jane in NY; Karen P., Amy E., Penny S., Paul B., and Roberto in IL; Jerry, Arlene, Karen N., Sheila, and Marilee in MN; Sandy B. in LA; Bob S. ("MTKN is my muse") and Alexandra in MI; AJ and Renee in MO; John C. in WI; Hank, Leighton, and Lori F. in IA; Bob C. and Amanda in DC; Kathy S. in WA; Laura W. in OR; Kendra, Matt B., and Kenn in CA; and Inez in ID. I'm proud to be among so many intelligent information professionals!

The best person I met through MySpace (don't laugh, it was a long time ago!), Marie W. in MA. All my best to you and Mark and your family!

And Lee, for those years when we were young, and the neighborhood was full of adventures to be had. Sometimes, just running around with the kids who lived down the street was the most fun we needed to have.

This collection is also in memory of Grandpa and Grandma Allen, and Grandpa and Grandma Burke, who are hopefully proud of me from wherever they are in the Great Beyond; Gerald, also known as Papa, who had to leave us far too soon; and my great-aunt Dot, and great-uncle Charlie, two of the most generous people I've had the good fortune to know.

Thank you to my proofreaders, Heather, Valerie C., and Kerry, for making me look better. For the record, they did not proofread these end pages.

The photo on the cover was taken in 1993 or 1994. I used Canva.com to modify the scanned photo for my cover design. Thanks to Joanna Penn for recommending Canva on her site, www.thecreativepenn.com.

I designed the back cover using a tutorial by Derek Murphy on his site, www.creativindie.com. Thanks to Derek for all the great resources and advice he shares with other indie authors.

About the Author

M. B. Manthe was born and raised in Massachusetts. She dropped out of high school when she turned sixteen, and began working in a local hospital. After earning her GED, she attended Community College of Rhode Island, then transferred to Smith College in Northampton, Massachusetts. She graduated in 1995 with a B.A. in English Language and Literature. She spent two years at the University of Arizona, completing her Master's degree in Library Science in December 1997. She lives in Topeka, Kansas, with her husband, two teenage sons, two dogs, two cats, over 1000 books, and never enough time to read as much as she'd like.

Visit her online (where she plans to post more often, she really does!) at www.allthepartsofmylife.com, or chat with her on Twitter, where she goes by @heathmocha.

www.ingramcontent.com/pod-product-compliance
Lightning Source LLC
Chambersburg PA
CBHW020622300426
44113CB00007B/752